YANKEE SHORTS

501 OF THE FUNNIEST ONE-LINERS

GLENN LIEBMAN

CONTEMPORARY BOOKS

Library of Congress Cataloging-in-Publication Data

Liebman, Glenn.
    Yankee shorts : 501 of the funniest one-liners / Glenn Liebman.
       p.   cm.
    ISBN 0-8092-2983-8
    1. New York Yankees (Baseball team)—Humor.   2. Baseball
players—United States—Quotations.   I. Title.
GV875.N4L54   1997
796.357′64′097471—dc21   97-20726
                                           CIP

Published by Contemporary Books
An imprint of NTC/Contemporary Publishing Company
4255 West Touhy Avenue, Lincolnwood (Chicago), Illinois 60646-1975 U.S.A.
Copyright © 1997 by Glenn Liebman
Manufactured in the United States of America
International Standard Book Number: 0-8092-2983-8

17   16   15   14   13   12   11   10   9   8   7   6   5   4   3   2   1

To Kathy and Frankie,
whose enthusiasm for life fills every day
with laughter, happiness, and anticipation

ACKNOWLEDGMENTS

I'd like to first thank my agent, Philip Spitzer, for his help with this book and the prior eight books in the Shorts series. I'd also like to thank Nancy Crossman, my former editor, for being such a great supporter. I'd also like to thank Alina Cowden, my current editor, for her intelligence and accessibility. And I would like to thank my friend Craig Bolt for his sense of humor and dedication to the entire Shorts series.

Thanks also to the individuals who made this book possible—the great characters of the Yankees, including Yogi, Babe, Casey, the Scooter, and so many more.

I'd also like to thank my friends who are Yankees fans, who thankfully have never been obnoxious when the Yankees win and the Mets lose: Jerry Klein, Scott Sommer, David and Joel Agler, David Wollner, Joe Vetrone, and Billy "Little Scooter" Hanft.

Thanks go to my mother-in-law, Helen Coll, for being a great fan of the books and a wonderful grandmother who buys her grandson every toy known to man. When people come over to our house, we have to remind them that we have only one child, not seven.

I'd like to thank my mother, Frieda, for giving me her sense of humor; my dad, Bernie, for teaching me his persistence; and my brother, Bennett, for teaching me about decency and how to read a racing form.

I'd like to thank my son, Frankie, for his enthusiasm, sense of humor, intelligence, and quick ability to grasp potty training.

Finally, as always, I'd like to thank my wife, Kathy, who has been my best friend for the last fourteen years and will be for at least the next forty. She is not only a wonderful wife but also the world's best mother. I'm lucky she is my partner.

INTRODUCTION

When you grow up in New York, it is almost pre-determined whether you will be a Yankees fan or a Mets fan. My father, being an ardent supporter of the Brooklyn Dodgers, guaranteed that I would grow up a Mets fan.

However, I must confess that over the last twenty years I have increasingly become a fan of the pinstripes.

The first hint of change came in 1976 when I was a freshman at Northeastern University in Boston. Everyone in my dorm was a Red Sox fan. As a New Yorker, I felt it was incumbent upon me to defend the pride of the Yankees. Back in '76, it was actually fun to root for a good team and classy players like Roy White and Chris Chambliss. After my years in Boston, my dislike of the Yankees turned into ambivalence.

The next change came in 1987 when I went to a baseball-card show where legendary Yankees Lefty

Gomez and Tommy Henrich were signing autographs. They were the funniest and nicest baseball
players I had ever met.

My mother and my brother were with me, and
Henrich spent half an hour talking to my mom
about New York in the 1940s. A few years later I
ran into Henrich at another card show and we
talked about my mom, who was very ill. He
remembered her and took the time to write a
special note to her about their earlier conversation.
How can you root against an organization that had
individuals like Old Reliable, Tommy Henrich?

The final metamorphosis that turned me into
a Yankees fan was the 1996 Yankees. Don't get me
wrong—I've never been a frontrunner (my lifelong
allegiance to the New York Jets proved that), but
how could you not root for that team?

Could you have scripted a more decent, com-
passionate manager than Joe Torre? Add selfless
players like Bernie Williams, Mariano Rivera, Jimmy
Key, and Derek Jeter and you have all the ingre-
dients for a team that only the most virulent
Yankees hater could dislike.

If the Yankees play the Mets in this year's
World Series, I will probably root for the Mets, but
without the self-assurance I once would have had.
This is quite a change for someone who once traded
all his Mickey Mantle and Whitey Ford cards for a
few Ed Kranepool and Ron Swoboda cards.

The other reason it has become fun to be a
Yankees fan is that to know about Yankees history is

to know about baseball history. No other team can come close to boasting such an awesome array of stars. Luckily, a lot of the Yankees greats were also the funniest people in baseball history.

Whether it's the Bambino, Yogi, the Yankee Clipper, the Old Professor, the Scooter, the Mick, Reggie, David Cone, or even George, the Yankees have shown us great skills on the field and provided us with great laughs off the diamond.

AGE OF INNOCENCE

"The older they get, the better they were when they were younger."

Jim Bouton, on Old-Timers' Day

"I'm still Reggie, but not so often."
Reggie Jackson, at age 38

"When your dentist's kid starts hitting you, it's time to go."

Tommy John, after Mark McGwire, the son of John's dentist, hit a home run off him

"He's the only guy we had who looked like Judge Wapner."

Dave LaPoint, on why 45-year-old Tommy John was put in charge of the Yankees' kangaroo court

"Old-timers' games, weekends, and airplane landings are alike. If you can walk away from them, they're successful."
Casey Stengel

"The trick is growing up without growing old."
Casey Stengel

"There comes a time in every man's life, and I've
had plenty of them."
Casey Stengel

"I'll never make the mistake of being 70 again."
*Casey Stengel, on being forced to
retire as the Yankees manager in
1960 at age 70*

"Sure, did you think I was born old?"
*Casey Stengel, when Mickey Mantle
asked if Stengel had ever played at
Ebbets Field*

ALL—STAR GAME

"They didn't call me Slick for nothing."
*Whitey Ford, on striking out Willie
Mays in the 1964 All-Star Game with
a spitter*

"I don't really go there to compete. I go there to be seen."

Reggie Jackson, on All-Star Games

"It's a lousy job. No matter who you pick, you're gonna be condemned."

Billy Martin, on being the All-Star Game manager

AUTOGRAPHS

" 'Sorry, Mickey,' the Lord said, 'but I wanted to give you the word personally. You can't go to heaven because of the way you acted down on earth, but would you mind signing a dozen baseballs?' "

Mickey Mantle, relating a recurring nightmare of his

"I love signing autographs. I'll sign anything but veal cutlets. My ballpoint pen slips on veal cutlets."

Casey Stengel

3

"I never saw the Babe make a mistake in a ball game. Ruth always knew, instinctively, what to do on a ballfield."

Ed Barrow

"I didn't room with him. I roomed with his suitcase."

Ping Bodie

"The only sports legend I ever saw who completely lived up to advance billing was Babe Ruth."

Jimmy Breslin

"He was like a damn animal. He had that instinct. They know when it's going to rain, things like that. Nature, that was Ruth."

Rube Bressler

"To try to capture Babe Ruth with cold statistics would be like trying to keep up with him on a night out."

Bill Broeg

"Baseball brains are not part of everybody's head. Babe Ruth had baseball brains."
Eddie Collins

"When you figured the things he did, and the way he lived and the way he played, you've got to figure he was more than an animal even. There was never anyone like him. He was a god."
Joe Dugan

"All the lies about him are true."
Jimmy Dykes

"It was a tough year for the Babe."
Whitey Ford, on breaking Ruth's World Series record of scoreless innings pitched in 1961, the same year that Roger Maris broke Ruth's home-run record

"I believe the sale of Ruth will ultimately strengthen the team."
Harry Frazee, Red Sox owner, after selling Ruth to the Yankees

"It was impossible to watch him at bat without expressing an emotion."
Paul Gallico

"Some twenty years ago, I stopped talking about the Babe for the simple reason that I realized that those who had never seen him didn't believe me."
Tommy Holmes

"If you cut that big slob in half, most of the concessions at Yankee Stadium would be pouring out."
Waite Hoyt

"God bless Mommy, God bless Daddy, and God bless Babe Ruth because he upped Daddy's paycheck by 15 to 40 percent."
Waite Hoyt, on the prayer he recommended that every player's children recite

"Babe Ruth could hit a ball so hard and so far that it was sometimes hard to believe your eyes."
Sad Sam Jones

"I always felt just like a kid at the circus whenever I saw him hit a home run."

Herb Pennock

"I've come to the rather hopeless conclusion that there isn't any way to fool Babe."

Ray Schalk, on the best way to pitch to Ruth

"He'd hit 'em so high that everyone on the field thought he had a chance to get it. They'd all try to get under it to make the catch, and it looked like a union meeting."

Casey Stengel, on pop flies hit by Ruth

BASEBALL WISDOM, YANKEE STYLE

"Baseball teams are like human beings. They are born, live, and die."

Edward Barrow, on occasional Yankees defeats

"You spend a good part of your life gripping a baseball, and it turns out it was the other way around all the time."
Jim Bouton

"Baseball players are smarter than football players. How often do you see a baseball team penalized for too many men on the field?"
Jim Bouton

"A ballplayer's got to be kept hungry to become a big leaguer. That's why no boy from a rich family ever made the big leagues."
Joe DiMaggio

"Baseball is a kid's game that grown-ups only tried to screw up."
Bob Lemon

"I've often thought that a lot of awards are made-up deals, so you'll come to the dinner."
Mickey Mantle

"I'm glad I don't play anymore. I could never learn all those handshakes."
Phil Rizzuto

"I've had many years that I was not so successful as a ballplayer, as it was a game of skill."
Casey Stengel

"The best thing to do is to have players who can hit right-handed and left-handed and hit farther one way and farther somehow the other way and run like the wind."
Casey Stengel, explaining his strategy for winning

"Now, there's three things you can do in a baseball game: You can win or you can lose or it can rain."
Casey Stengel

BEVERAGE OF CHOICE

"I did pass the bar. But as some might say, I haven't passed one since."
Mel Allen, legendary Yankees announcer, on his days in law school

"So would the Babe."

> *Waite Hoyt, pallbearer at Ruth's*
> *funeral, responding to Joe Dugan, a*
> *fellow pallbearer, who said that he'd*
> *give a hundred dollars for a beer*

"I had bad days on the field. But I didn't take them home with me. I left them in a bar along the way home."

> *Bob Lemon*

"They say that some of my stars drink whiskey, but I have found that the ones who drink milk shakes don't win many ball games."

> *Casey Stengel*

BILLY BALL

"Playing for Yogi is like playing for your father; playing for Billy is like playing for your father-in-law."

> *Don Baylor, on the difference*
> *between Yogi Berra and Billy Martin*

"Lots of people look up to Billy Martin. That's because he just knocked them down."

Jim Bouton

"Charles Finley hiring Billy Martin is like Captain Hook hiring the alligator."

Johnny Carson

"He'll beat you any way he can. He'll kick you, and bite you, cut you, knock your brains out if he can."

Charlie Dressen, on Martin as a player

"I can tell you Billy has a great heart, but I can't vouch for his liver."

Whitey Ford

"Better Billy Martin than Dick Howser."

Dick Howser, on Martin being hired back for the fourth time as Yankees manager

"He's the kind of guy you'd like to kill if he's playing for the other team, but you'd like ten of them on your side."

Frank Lane, on Martin

"You know, this is like having Billy Martin in your pocket."

Mickey Mantle, on using a device on the golf course that utters curses at the push of a button

"I don't throw the first punch. I throw the next four."

Billy Martin

"His teams don't have any particular style. That's why he's so good. The first thing you notice is that no two of his teams are alike."

Earl Weaver, on Martin

BIRD CALL

"I knew it was dead, so I just reached down and put it in my glove. I mean, I wasn't gonna give him mouth-to-beak resuscitation."

> *Bill LaMacchia, Brewers ballboy,*
> *after a Rickey Henderson fly ball hit*
> *a bird*

WADE BOGGS

"I think that when he comes to the plate, he should only get one swing."

> *Greg Gagne*

BOOK BEAT

"Yeah, what paper you write for, Ernie?"

> *Yogi Berra, upon meeting Ernest*
> *Hemingway and being told he was*
> *a writer*

"How'd your book come out?"

> *Yogi Berra, to teammate Dr. Bobby Brown, who was reading* Gray's Anatomy *while Yogi was reading a comic book*

"I thought if I ever get to be famous or great I'd write about it. Unfortunately, I couldn't wait any longer."

> *Jim Bouton, on writing* Ball Four

"I read Billy Martin's autobiography, and when I woke up the next day, I beat the hell out of my pillow."

> *Lefty Gomez*

"Before he writes a book, he's got to read one."

> *Dallas Green, after Rickey Henderson threatened to write a tell-all book about the Yankees*

"I guess I could have written two books about my life—one for the adults and one for the kids."

> *Babe Ruth*

14

THE BOSS

"It was a beautiful sight to behold, with all 36 oars working in unison."

> *Jack Buck, on George*
> *Steinbrenner's yacht*

"If we lose eight or nine games in a row, I'm not going to jump into the same elevator with Steinbrenner."

> *Dave Collins, after signing with the*
> *Yankees as a free agent*

"I think he should stay up in his office, push his buttons, count his money, and stay out of the locker room."

> *Dock Ellis*

"As soon as I get there, I'm going to rip Steinbrenner just to get it out of the way."

> *Mickey Hatcher, responding to*
> *rumors he was being traded to*
> *the Yankees*

"Why would George Steinbrenner want me? Did he fire his limo driver?"

Mickey Hatcher

"I tell George what I think and then I do what he says."

Bob Lemon

"I understand exactly how you must have felt in that elevator. I only hope you don't have a good-behavior clause in your contract."

Telegram Billy Martin sent to Steinbrenner after Steinbrenner's alleged fight during the '81 World Series

"Nothing is more limited than being a limited partner of George's."

John McMullen, on being a partial owner of the Yankees

"I don't know, but if he does, I want to be the owner."

Gene Michael, asked if George could ever be a big-league manager

"Believe it or not, he hasn't won anything for us yet. The players and the managers and coaches have actually won the games."

Graig Nettles, on Steinbrenner's leadership skills

"There are two things Steinbrenner knows nothing about—baseball and weight control."

Graig Nettles

"When George came into the clubhouse, you shook and shivered."

Phil Niekro, comparing Ted Turner to George Steinbrenner

"George is always trying to patch up the tire when the car needs a new set of wheels."

Lou Piniella

"The two biggest expenses for the Yankee employees are coming and going-away parties."

Bob Quinn, former Yankees GM

"How do you know when George Steinbrenner is lying? When you see his lips move."

Jerry Reinsdorf

"Every time you go into his office, he greets you warmly and shakes you by the throat."
>
> *Al Rosen*

"George Steinbrenner knows nothing about baseball. He doesn't understand that this is a major-league team, not Purdue."
>
> *Jim Spencer*

"In the end, I'll win. I always do."
>
> *George Steinbrenner, on his disenchantment with Lou Piniella as manager of the Yankees*

"My heel felt just like George Steinbrenner: irritating, painful, nagging, and wouldn't go away."
>
> *Mychal Thompson, basketball player, on a heel injury*

"If the fight really took place the way George says it did, this is the first time a millionaire has ever hit someone and not been sued."
>
> *Edward Bennett Williams, on Steinbrenner's alleged 1981 elevator fight*

"He has nothin' to do with nothin'."
Dave Winfield

CATFISH

"He puts the ball right where he wants it. It looks easy until you try to hit it."
Reggie Jackson, on Catfish Hunter

"I've never seen a guy who gets more out of less natural ability than Catfish Hunter. It's an education just to watch him."
Rudy May

COACH

"The best qualification a coach can have is being the manager's drinking buddy."
Jim Bouton

"What the Yankees need is a second-base coach."
Graig Nettles, on poor baserunning by the Yankees

"When I'm feeling good, I'm a player. When I'm feeling bad, I'm a coach."

> *Lou Piniella, on being a*
> *Yankees player/coach*

COLUMBUS

"This is the only town in baseball where you have to call the roll every day."

> *Bucky Dent, manager of Columbus,*
> *on the many call-ups made by the*
> *Yankees during a pennant race*

"I don't want to be in your future. It's frustrating enough being in your present."

> *Roger Erickson, on retiring*
> *from baseball after being*
> *demoted to Columbus*

"LaRoche is like *The Sporting News*. He comes out once a week."

> *Graig Nettles, on Dave LaRoche*
> *shuttling between the Yankees*
> *and Columbus*

EARLE COMBS

"We've got a couple of guys named Babe Ruth and Bob Meusel who hit the ball a long way. You get on base and wait for them to knock you in."

Miller Huggins, on calling Earle Combs "The Waiter"

COMMISSIONER

" 'Great Sea Stories by the Captain of the Titanic.' "

George Steinbrenner, suggesting a title for Bowie Kuhn's autobiography

"Who in their right mind would accept a job with George Steinbrenner, Ted Turner, and Marge Schott's dog as your boss?"

Peter Ueberroth, on being commissioner of baseball

DAVID CONE

"David Cone is in a class by himself with three or four other players."
George Steinbrenner

CY YOUNG AWARD

"I'm going to build a glass case on my front lawn with a big spotlight and display it."
Sparky Lyle, after winning the
Cy Young Award

"From Cy Young to sayonara in one season."
Graig Nettles, on Sparky Lyle
winning the Cy Young Award in
1977 and then being traded after
the '78 season

DAY GAMES

"It gets late early out there."

Yogi Berra, on the shadows in
Yankee Stadium

"In the daytime, you sat in the dugout and talked about women. At night you went out with women and talked about baseball."

Waite Hoyt, on baseball in the
old days

DEE—FENSE

"Did he bring his glove, too?"

Anonymous, after being told that
poor fielder Cliff Johnson took his
bat to church to get it blessed

"You don't go when you hear the crack of the bat, you go before you hear it."

Joe DiMaggio, on his great
outfield instincts

"Catching a fly ball is a pleasure, but knowing what to do with it after you catch it is a business."
Tommy Henrich

"Blind men find acorns once in a while."
Reggie Jackson, on a good defensive play he made

"We go over positioning for relays and bunt plays. Then we play Hangman."
Dave LaRoche, Yankees coach, on why he uses a blackboard to detail defensive strategies

"It's not that Reggie is a bad outfielder. He just has trouble judging the ball and picking it up."
Billy Martin, on Jackson's fielding problems

"I said you were an average outfielder."
Jim Palmer, to Reggie Jackson, backtracking from calling Jackson a mediocre outfielder

"In center field, you've got too much time to think about everything but baseball."

> *Joe Pepitone, on why he didn't like the outfield*

"I don't like those fellas who drive in two runs and let in three."

> *Casey Stengel*

"Bobby Brown reminds me of a fellow who's been hitting for 12 years and fielding one."

> *Casey Stengel*

DESIGNATED HITTER

"With Bobby Bonds in right field and three first basemen, I might as well donate my glove to charity."

> *Ron Blomberg, on being baseball's first designated hitter*

"Well, sometimes my body feels 60."

> *Ron Blomberg, after Carlton Fisk said that being a designated hitter is for someone who's 60 years old*

DIAMOND IN THE ROUGH

"I wanted to find out if the diamond was real, so I cut the glass on my coffee table with it. Then I found out that the coffee table was worth more than the ring."

> *Sparky Lyle, on the rings George*
> *Steinbrenner gave the Yankees for*
> *winning the '77 World Series*

BILL DICKEY

"Dickey is teaching me his experiences."

> *Yogi Berra, on being groomed as*
> *Dickey's successor*

"Dickey isn't just a catcher. He's a ball club. He isn't just a player. He's an influence."

> *Dan Daniel, sportswriter*

"I can't remember your name. But I know we used to pitch you high and outside."

> *Bill Dickey, after Joe Gantenbein*
> *asked if Dickey remembered him*

DOCTOR IN THE HOUSE

"He's trying to make enough money to pay the first premium on his malpractice insurance."
Dick Howser, on Doc Medich

"He had such lousy hands when he played third, I wouldn't want him operating on me."
Gene Woodling, on Dr. Bobby Brown

DOCTOR K

"I'll stick to my job."
Wayne Gretzky, asked if he would like to face a Dwight Gooden fastball

DODGERS

"I predicted they'd win it in six."

> *Billy Loes, Dodgers pitcher,*
> *claiming that he was misquoted*
> *when he said the Yankees would*
> *beat the Dodgers in seven games in*
> *the 1953 World Series*

"The key to beating the Dodgers is to keep them from hugging each other too much."

> *Graig Nettles, on the Dodgers during*
> *the Tommy Lasorda era*

RYNE DUREN

"Ryne Duren was a one-pitch pitcher. His one pitch was a wild warm-up."

> *Jim Bouton*

"I would not advise hitting against Duren, because if he ever hit you in the head you might be in the past tense."

> *Casey Stengel*

"I've always wished that if the good Lord ever let us win the World Series, it would be against these Yankees who beat us twice."

> *Tom Lasorda, after the Dodgers won the '81 World Series in six games*

"If somebody has kicked your butt twice, you want the chance to kick his."

> *Davey Lopes, on why beating the Yankees felt so good*

"Steinbrenner is sending the entire team on an all-expense-paid trip to the Bermuda Triangle."

> *Scott Ostler, sportswriter, after the Yankees lost the Series by dropping four straight*

"I'm going to come out and play like there's no tomorrow."

> *Willie Randolph, said just before Game 6 of the Series*

EL GOOFY

"Clean living and a fast outfield."
>*Lefty Gomez, on how he achieved a*
>*great World Series record*

EXTRA INNINGS

"It's like playing a doubleheader without anything to eat between games."
>*Roy White, after the Yankees lost in*
>*18 innings to the Senators*

FAMILY

"I was nearly an orphan myself. I had only one mother and one father."
>*Joe Dugan*

"I asked my son if he could have his daughter call me 'Uncle.'"

> *Mickey Mantle, on being a*
> *grandfather at age 57*

FASTBALLS

"Nobody knows how fast I am. The ball doesn't get to the mitt that often."

> *Lefty Gomez*

CECIL FIELDER

"It could be worse. He could be in Detroit."

> *David Cone, on Fielder wanting to be*
> *traded because of his part-time status*
> *on the Yankees*

"The Fat Albert balloon sprung a leak and at the last minute was replaced by Yankee first baseman Cecil Fielder."

> *David Letterman, on the*
> *Macy's Thanksgiving Day Parade*

"I couldn't'a done it without my players."

> *Casey Stengel, on being heaped with*
> *praise following the Yankees' winning*
> *of the '58 World Series*

FINES

"If this club wants somebody to play third, they've got me. If they want somebody to go to luncheons, they should hire George Jessel."

> *Graig Nettles, on being fined $500*
> *for missing a charity event*

"Nobody told me nothing. I knew there were sign-ups, but I didn't see them."

> *Ruben Sierra, on not showing up for*
> *the Yankees team picture*

"There are close to 11 million unemployed, and half of them are New York managers."

Johnny Carson

"You know, throughout the World Series, it was really a team victory, and the team played so well. George Steinbrenner is really not sure who he's going to fire."

David Letterman, after the Yankees won the '96 World Series

"The only real way to know you're fired is when you arrive at the ballpark and find your name has been scratched from the parking list."

Billy Martin

"All I know is I pass people on the street these days, and they don't know whether to say hello or to say good-bye."

Billy Martin, on his tenuous status as Yankees manager

"Now I know how Truman felt when he dropped that bomb."

> *Billy Martin, on the pressure of being fired*

"If you're the Yankees manager with the team on a road trip, you'd be wise not to send out your laundry."

> *Phil Rizzuto*

"If you lose five in a row in New York, the general manager gets fired. Here he gets a lifetime contract."

> *John Wathan, Royals catcher, after Royals GM John Schuerholz was given a lifetime contract during a five-game losing streak*

FLAKES

"When we broke camp this spring, I fined Shirley for making the club."

> *Don Baylor, on noted flake Bob Shirley joining the Yankees*

"The trouble with Cowley is that he's in his own world and we're just visiting it."
Don Baylor, on Joe Cowley

"I went to the mound to take him out and he told me, 'Good move, Skip.' In all the years I've been managing, no pitcher has told me that."
Billy Martin, on Cowley

FOOD FOR THOUGHT

"OK, but no potatoes. I'm on a diet."
Yogi Berra, asked if he wanted french fries

"No, the meat's too tough, and the horns get stuck in my teeth."
Yogi Berra, asked when he was in Alaska if he wanted mousse for dessert

"It was hard to have a conversation with anyone. There were so many people talking."
Yogi Berra, after attending a White House dinner

"You learn to eat rice in a hurry."

David Cone, on spending $150 for
a steak in Japan

'41 WORLD SERIES

"That was a tough break for poor Mickey to get.
I bet he feels like a nickel's worth of dog meat."

Tommy Henrich, on the famous
passed ball of Mickey Owens after
Henrich struck out, a miscue that
kept the inning alive and allowed the
Yankees to ultimately win Game 4 of
the Series

GEORGE AND BILLY

"A fatal attraction."

Reggie Jackson, on the Martin-
Steinbrenner relationship

"There's an idea that's always worked well in the past. It's like Gary Hart trying to patch things up with Donna Rice."

Mike Lupica, on Steinbrenner hiring Martin for the fifth time

"It's a lot better than most people think. Actually, we're the same in many ways. The only difference is he's rich and I'm poor."

Billy Martin, on his relationship with Steinbrenner

"Those two shy from the spotlight like moths."
Scott Ostler, sportswriter

"George and Billy and me are two of a kind."
Mickey Rivers

GEORGE AND REGGIE

"George is making it worse. He's been on me. I used to be 6′2″; now I'm 5′9″."

Reggie Jackson, on the abuse he was getting during the '81 playoffs against the Brewers

"The two of them deserve each other. One's a born liar, the other's convicted."

> *Billy Martin, on Reggie Jackson and George Steinbrenner*

GOOD OLD USA

"Yeah, only in America can a thing like that happen."

> *Yogi Berra, on a Jewish mayor being elected in Dublin, Ireland*

GOOSE

"I was out mowing my lawn during the baseball strike. I got the front yard done and about half the back, and then I kept waiting for Goose Gossage to run out and finish it for me."

> *Tommy John, on the relief work of Gossage*

"He can make the ball look so small that you're not even sure there's a practical reason for being up there."

John Lowenstein, on Gossage

"Gossage puts guys like me on his cereal for breakfast. He's the most intimidating pitcher I've ever seen."

Tom Paciorek

"You feel guilty telling the batters to go out there and get a hit. They look at you funny, as if to say, 'You try it.'"

Earl Weaver, on managing a team facing Gossage

"When he's out there on the mound, he scares the devil out of you."

Richie Zisk, on why he calls Gossage "The Exorcist"

"Best accuracy I've ever seen from 25 feet away."
Ralph Houk, on the tobacco-
spitting prowess of Yankees pitcher
Thad Tillotson

GREED

"I think greed is a terrible thing—unless you're in on the ground floor."
Yogi Berra

"He's a good kid, but he's not that little old farm boy from the banks of the Wabash anymore. He's just like the rest of them. He's out for the almighty buck."
George Steinbrenner, on Don
Mattingly's 1987 arbitration hearing

GUN CONTROL

"Whenever I decided to release a guy, I always had his room searched for a gun. You couldn't take any chances with some of them birds."

Casey Stengel

HAIR IT IS

"It's like I used to tell my barber. Shave and a haircut, but don't cut my throat. I may want to do that myself."

Casey Stengel

"I call it 'The Watergate'; I cover up everything I can."

Joe Torre, on his hairstyle

HALL OF FAME

"It seems strange to me that some fellows have passed me on the ballot without any of us getting any more hits."

> *Johnny Mize, on having to wait*
> *several years before being elected to*
> *the Hall of Fame*

"I'll take any way to get into the Hall of Fame. If they want a batboy, I'll go in as a batboy."
> *Phil Rizzuto*

"It shows what you can accomplish if you stay up all night drinking whiskey all the time."

> *Toots Shor, famed restaurant owner,*
> *on the induction of Mickey Mantle*
> *and Whitey Ford into the Hall of*
> *Fame in 1974*

"No one in the history of baseball has ever had more of an offensive influence in a game than Rickey."

> *Gene Michael, on the greatness of Rickey Henderson*

HITTING

"You can't bat and think at the same time."
> *Yogi Berra*

"That's his style of hitting. If you can't imitate him, don't copy him."
> *Yogi Berra, on Frank Robinson's hitting style*

"For the first time in twenty years, I broke a bat the other day. Backed my car over it in the garage."
> *Lefty Gomez, on his weak hitting*

"The key to hitting is relaxing, not brute strength. If it were brute strength, Hulk Hogan would lead the league in everything."
Lou Piniella

HOME—RUN DERBY

"The fans would rather see me hit one homer to right than three doubles to left."
Babe Ruth

"He hit it a lot further than it went."
Curt Young, on a Rickey Henderson home run

HORSE SENSE

"Steinbrenner fired the horse and then had Billy Martin run in the Preakness."
Chris Berman, after Steinbrenner's horse Eternal Princess finished 12th in the Kentucky Derby

"I like my horses better because they can't talk to sportswriters."

George Steinbrenner, comparing his players to his horses

ELSTON HOWARD

"The Yankees lost more class on the weekend than George Steinbrenner could buy in ten years."

Red Smith, on the death of Elston Howard

INJURY LIST

"Back then, if you had a sore arm, the only people concerned were you and your wife. Now it's you, your wife, your agent, your investment counselor, your stockbroker, and your publisher."

Jim Bouton

"I have mixed emotions. I think I may have been in line for Player of the Month in the Florida State League."

> *Tommy John, on being called up to the Yankees in mid-August after rehabilitation of an arm injury*

"My goals are to hit .300, score 100 runs, and stay injury prone."

> *Mickey Rivers*

INSTANT REPLAY

"There are no replays at the ballpark."

> *Ambrosio Sojo, father of Luis Sojo, on why he watches games on television rather than going to games*

INTELLIGENCE TESTS

"Every time I was voted Manager of the Year, I got dumb over the winter and got fired in June."

> *Bob Lemon*

"The kid is the greatest proof of reincarnation. Nobody could be that stupid in one lifetime."

> *Joe McCarthy, on a player trying to steal home with one out*

IRON HORSE

"Today, I consider myself the luckiest man on the face of the earth."

> *Lou Gehrig, his famous words said on Lou Gehrig Day, July 4, 1939*

"It's a pretty big shadow. It gives me lots of room to spread myself."

> *Lou Gehrig, on playing in the shadow of Ruth*

"Hell, Lou, it took 15 years to get you out of the game. Sometimes I'm out in 15 minutes."

> *Lefty Gomez, on Gehrig's streak of 2,130 consecutive games played*

"I didn't think a guy could be that good. Every time I looked up, that big guy was on base or flying by me on a homer."

Charlie Grimm, after Gehrig hit .529
in the 1932 World Series

"We never threw at Gehrig. You didn't want to get him mad. Best let him sleep."

Lefty Grove

"My name is linked with the great and courageous Lou Gehrig. I'm truly humbled to have our names spoken in the same breath."

Cal Ripken, on breaking Gehrig's
consecutive-game streak

JOBS

"I'd rather be a Yankee catcher than the president, and that makes me pretty lucky, I guess, because I could never be the president."

Yogi Berra

"I'm a vice president in charge of special marketing. That means I play golf and go to cocktail parties. I'm pretty good at my job."
>> *Mickey Mantle, on his job in*
>> *Atlantic City*

"It's a business. If I could make more money down in the zinc mine, I'd be mining zinc."
>> *Roger Maris*

JUST SAY NO

"I don't want to say much—just that it's a joke and it stinks."
>> *Butch Wynegar, Yankees catcher, on*
>> *Commissioner Ueberroth's drug policy*

JIM KAAT

"I'll never be considered one of the all-time greats, maybe not even one of the all-time goods. But I'm one of the all-time survivors."
>> *Jim Kaat*

"Kaat's baseball card, on the back, is all printed in microfilm, he's been around so long."

> Bill Lee, on the lengthy career
> of Kaat

KINGDOME

"In this ballpark, I feel that when you're walking to the plate, you're in scoring position."

> Don Baylor, on the first time he saw
> the Kingdome as the Yankee DH

KNUCKLER

"They might make me an honorary Niekro. Then they might let me pitch until I'm 80."

> Tommy John, on learning the
> knuckleball while a member of
> the Yankees

"Use a big glove and a pair of rosary beads."

> Joe Torre, on the best way to catch
> a knuckleball

LEFT—HANDERS

"Left-handers have more enthusiasm for life. They sleep on the wrong side of the bed, and their heads get more stagnant on that side."
Casey Stengel

LITTLE LEAGUE

"I think it's wonderful. It keeps the kids out of the house."
Yogi Berra, on why he's a fan of Little League

LOOKS MAKE THE MAN

"Well, I used to look like this when I was young, and now I still do."
Yogi Berra, on his youthful appearance

"He's so ugly, he should have to wear an oxygen mask."

Mickey Rivers, on a fellow Yankee

LOSING

"I wish I had an answer to that, because I'm getting tired of answering that question."

Yogi Berra, on explaining the Yankees' poor record

"We lost 13 straight one year. I decided if we got rained out, we'd have a victory party."

Lefty Gomez, on his minor-league managing days

"If there is such a thing as a good loser, then the game is crooked."

Billy Martin

"When I lose a ball game, I can't eat. Sometimes I can hardly sleep. If you're in love with the game, you can't turn it off and on like a light."

Billy Martin

"Most ball games are lost, not won."
Casey Stengel

LOUISIANA LIGHTNING

"What we need is Guidry and three days of rest."
*Sparky Lyle, on Ron Guidry, during
the Yankees' pennant drive in 1978*

"If you saw that pitching too often, there would be
a lot of guys doing different jobs."
Joe Rudi, on Ron Guidry

"If it was a home run for us, George Steinbrenner would have Maier on the Throgs Neck Bridge dangling somewhere."

> *Bobby Bonilla, Orioles player, after*
> *Maier, a 12-year-old Yankees fan,*
> *deflected a ball in the bleachers that*
> *was ruled a home run for the*
> *Yankees during the 1996 ALCS*
> *against the Orioles*

"If the kid keeps playing like he did last night, he's going to be a DH, I'll tell you that."

> *Reggie Jackson, on Maier deflecting*
> *the ball but being unable to catch it*

"It was a pretty high hit. I'm not used to seeing a ball hit that high in Little League."

> *Jeff Maier*

═══════════════════════════════

"Our similarities are different."

> *Dale Berra, on his father Yogi*

"Well, he'll have to call up a blacksmith."

> *Yogi Berra, upon hearing that Billy*
> *Martin had locked his keys in the car*

"You observe a lot just by watching."

> *Yogi Berra*

"Thanks. You don't look so hot yourself."

> *Yogi Berra, said to Mayor John*
> *Lindsay's wife after she commented*
> *that he looked cool in his suit*

"I really didn't say everything I said."

> *Yogi Berra*

"It's like déjà vu all over again."

> *Yogi Berra*

"I'd say he's done more than that."
>*Yogi Berra, asked if he thought Don*
>*Mattingly exceeded expectations*

"Public speaking is one of the best things I hate."
>*Yogi Berra*

"If the people don't want to come out to the park, nobody's going to stop them."
>*Yogi Berra*

"No one goes there anymore. It's too crowded."
>*Yogi Berra, on a popular restaurant*

"How do I know? I'm not in shape yet."
>*Yogi Berra, on his cap size*

"Pitching is 80 percent of the game. The other half is hitting and fielding."
>*Mickey Rivers*

"I might have to commute. You know, left field, DH, wherever."
>*Mickey Rivers, confusing commuting*
>*with platooning*

"We'll do all right if we can capitalize on
our mistakes."

Mickey Rivers

"There were other cities besides the Garden State
who wanted the Yankees."

Phil Rizzuto, on the Yankees'
rumored move to New Jersey

"I want to thank all my players for giving me the
honor of being what I was."

Casey Stengel

"All right, everyone line up alphabetically
according to your height."

Casey Stengel

"Winfield robbed Armas of at least a home run."

Bill White, during his days as a
Yankees announcer, calling a Tony
Armas at bat

MANAGING

"A good ball club."

> *Yogi Berra, asked what makes a*
> *good manager*

"A nervous breakdown with a big weekly
paycheck."

> *Bucky Dent, description of managing*
> *the Yankees*

"I was no genius. If you don't have the players, you
can't win."

> *Bucky Harris*

"If the players play good, I'll be smart. If they
don't play good, I'll probably be fired."

> *Bob Lemon*

"When I get through managing, I'm going to open
up a kindergarten."

> *Billy Martin*

"I believe if God had ever managed, he would have been very aggressive, the way I manage."
Billy Martin

"You can't freeze the ball in this game. You have to play till the last man is out."
Joe McCarthy

"Just about three things—a good memory, patience, and being able to recognize ability. You've got to be able to recognize ability—it's so damned important."
Joe McCarthy, on the key to managing well

"The secret of managing a club is to keep the five guys who hate you from the five who are undecided."
Casey Stengel

"What's the secret to platooning? You put a right-hand hitter against a left-hand pitcher, a left-hand batter against a right-hand pitcher, and on a cloudy day you use a fastball pitcher."
Casey Stengel

"What the hell is it but telling the umpire who's gonna play and then watching them play."
Casey Stengel, on managing

ROGER MARIS

"We're not even going to catch Roger Maris."
Whitey Herzog, on poor power numbers by the Cardinals

"I have nothing to be ashamed of. He hit 60 others, didn't he?"
Tracy Stallard, on giving up Maris's 61st homer

MARRIAGE

"Nobody can be a success in two national pastimes."
Jimmy Cannon, on the breakup of the marriage of Joe DiMaggio and Marilyn Monroe

"It was better than rooming with Joe Page."
>> *Joe DiMaggio, on his marriage to*
>> *Marilyn Monroe*

M A R S E   J O E

"McCarthy, even drinking, was six innings ahead of everybody else."
>> *Babe Dahlgren, on Yankees manager*
>> *Joe McCarthy*

"An Einstein in flannels."
>> *Lefty Gomez, on McCarthy*

"I hated McCarthy's guts, but there never was a better manager."
>> *Joe Page*

DON MATTINGLY

"It's hard to play the outfield with him hitting, because you find yourself so fascinated."
Dave Collins, on the impressive hitting style of Mattingly

"He's the best hitter I've ever seen. That's all there is to say about it."
Scott MacGregor

MEDIA BLITZ

"I can remember a reporter asking for a quote, and I didn't know what a quote was. I thought it was some kind of soft drink."
Joe DiMaggio, on his rookie year

"To hell with sportswriters. You can buy any of them with a steak."
George Weiss, longtime Yankees GM

METS

"It just shows you how easy this business is."
*Casey Stengel, after the Mets beat the
Yankees in an exhibition game in the
Mets' first year*

THE MICK

"Mickey Mantle can hit just as good right-handed
as he can left-handed. He's just naturally
amphibious."
Yogi Berra

"The body of a god. Only Mantle's legs are
mortal."
Jerry Coleman

"Everybody who roomed with Mickey said it took
five years off their career."
Whitey Ford

"Son, nobody is half as good as Mickey Mantle."

*Al Kaline, to a taunting fan who
said Kaline was not half as good
as Mickey Mantle*

"I always loved the game, but when my legs
weren't hurting, it was a lot easier to love."

Mickey Mantle

"Mickey Mantle is like me. We ain't like nobody."

Satchel Paige

"I was glad it hit the roof, because if it didn't, it
would have traveled another six miles."

*Pedro Ramos, on Mantle hitting a
ball off Ramos that was within six
inches of leaving Yankee Stadium*

"The day Mickey Mantle bunted when the wind was
blowing out in Crosley Field."

*Robin Roberts, asked to name his
greatest All-Star Game thrill*

"The big thing about this boy is he likes to play baseball. The knees bother him and he still comes to me and says, 'Let me play.'"

Casey Stengel

"He was the best one-legged player I ever saw play the game."

Casey Stengel

"Mickey tried to hit every one like they didn't count under four hundred feet."

Casey Stengel

"That kid hits them pretty far. The stratmosphere around here helps. . . . But you still gotta be pretty good to hit them that way."

Casey Stengel

MICK THE QUICK

"Rivers was the person least likely to be the chancellor of anything."

Graig Nettles, on why he nicknamed
Mickey Rivers "The Chancellor"

MISTER NOVEMBER

"I hit a home run once in November, in the
Instructional League."

> *Reggie Jackson, on the possibility of*
> *Mr. October having to play in a*
> *World Series game in November*

MONEY TREE

"If the guy was real poor, I'd give it back to him."

> *Yogi Berra, asked what he would do*
> *if he found a million dollars*

"A nickel ain't worth a dime anymore."

> *Yogi Berra, on his dime-store*
> *philosophy*

"My father looked at the check and then told the
scout, 'Throw in another hundred and you can
take the rest of the family.'"

> *Joe Dugan, on signing with the*
> *Yankees for a $500 contract in the*
> *early 1920s*

"If I want to meet millionaires, all I have to do is visit my locker room."

> *George Steinbrenner, declining an invitation to a luncheon with a group of millionaires*

MOVIES WITH YOGI

"He must have made that before he died."

> *Yogi Berra, on a Steve McQueen movie*

"It reminds me of being in the Army, even though I was in the Navy."

> *Yogi Berra, on* Biloxi Blues

"You should see the last fifteen minutes of the movie. I couldn't even see it."

> *Yogi Berra, on* Fatal Attraction

"Oh, what's the matter with you now?"

> *Yogi Berra, after his wife said she was going to see* Dr. Zhivago

THURMAN MUNSON

"He's not moody, he's just mean. When you're moody, you're nice sometimes."
Sparky Lyle, on Munson

"I think he'd play with a bullet in his leg."
Billy Martin, on Munson's toughness

MURDERER'S ROW

"You can never have too much talent. Even the 1927 Yankees didn't win every year."
Buzzie Bavasi

"Let's go out on the ballfield and hope we don't all get killed."
Donie Bush, Pirates manager, on facing the 1927 Yankees in the World Series

"It's always the same. Combs walks. Koenig singles. Ruth hits one out of the park. Gehrig doubles. Lazzeri triples. Then Dugan goes in the dirt on his can."

Joe Dugan, on the lineup of the '27 Yankees

"The Yankees not only beat the tar out of you, they tear your heart out. I wish the season was over right now so we wouldn't have to play them anymore."

Joe Judge, Senators player, on the '27 Yankees

"It isn't a race in the American League, it's a landslide."

John Kieran, New York Times reporter, on the '27 Yankees leading by 11½ games by July 4

"One of them had me dead already."

Mark Koenig, in his eighties, on why he didn't trust books written about the '27 Yankees

NERVES

"Have you ever pitched in front of 60,000 people with the bases loaded?"

> *George Frazier, asked if he was*
> *nervous playing in the '81 playoffs*

GRAIG NETTLES

"Never saw defense like that in my life. He won the World Series for us in that one game."

> *Bucky Dent, on the fielding of*
> *Graig Nettles in Game 3 of the*
> *'78 World Series*

"I get sick to my stomach watching Nettles make those plays. He must go to bed hoping and praying he can kill us with his glove."

> *Tom Lasorda, on the fielding of*
> *Nettles against the Dodgers*

"As impenetrable as the Italian Alps in front of anything hit down to or in the general vicinity of third base."

Jim Murray, on Nettles

"I expect every ball to be hit to me. When I do that, I'm never surprised."

Graig Nettles

NEW YORK, NEW YORK

"I could never play in New York. The first time I ever came into a game there, I got into the bull pen car and they told me to lock the doors."

Mike Flanagan

"They told me to watch out for sharks. I saw a lot of bodies, but no sharks."

Bob Shirley, on his first boat ride around New York after being acquired by the Yankees

"That borough of churches and bad ball clubs, many of which I had."

Casey Stengel, on Brooklyn

"It actually giggles at you as it goes by."
                    Rick Monday, on Niekro's knuckler

"Trying to hit him is like trying to eat Jell-O
with chopsticks."
                    Bobby Murcer, on Niekro

"First I found it hard to catch him. Then I found
it hard to hit him. And finally I found it hard to
manage him."
                    Joe Torre, on Niekro

'96 WORLD SERIES

"No longer is this team playing against the
overmatched Yankees. The Braves are playing
against history."
                    Mark Bradley, columnist, Atlanta
                    Constitution, *after the Braves won
                    the first two games of the Series*

"Once upon a time, we scribes scribbled over Yankee stories with pens fashioned from razor wire. Now we tickle the keyboards with feathers."

Dave Kindred, on the 1996 Yankees being regarded as good guys as well as champions

"We don't have Dom [Perignon] yet, but that's the next step."

Jim Leyritz, drinking wine after the Yankees beat the Orioles in the 1996 American League Championship Series

"The Yankees win the World Series. Maybe there will be another team like it someday. It will have to be some team. One of those forever teams."

Mike Lupica

"It's like watching someone else eat a hot-fudge sundae. And that's not fun."

Joe Torre, on waiting 4,272 games as a player and a manager before reaching the World Series

NO – HITTER

"This is not even close to the way I envisioned a no-hitter would be."

> *Andy Hawkins, after pitching a*
> *no-hitter and losing 4–0 due to three*
> *errors in the eighth inning*

NOBEL PRIZE

"I just won the Nobel prize of baseball."

> *Elston Howard, on winning the 1963*
> *American League MVP award*

"They should give Billy Martin the Nobel Peace Prize for managing."

> *Reggie Jackson, on managing the*
> *'77 Yankees*

NUMBERS GAME

"Better make it four. I don't think I can eat eight."
Yogi Berra, asked if he wanted his
pizza cut into four or eight slices

"I know my days are numbered. I just don't know the numbers."
Rudy May, near the end of his career
with the Yankees

OLD PROFESSOR

"It's the first role I ever played in a foreign language."
Charles Durning, on portraying
Casey Stengel in a one-man show

"If he turned pro, he'd put us all out of business."
George Gobel, comedian, on the
comic talents of Stengel

"A competitor who always had fun competing, a fighter with a gift of laughter."
Red Smith, on Stengel

"I was such a dangerous hitter, I even got intentional walks in batting practice."
Casey Stengel, on his playing days

"If you walk backwards, you'll find out that you can go forwards and people won't know if you're coming or going."
Casey Stengel

"They've got two languages I never learned to speak—French and English."
Casey Stengel, on why he never visited Montreal

OLD RELIABLE

"That guy can hit me in the middle of the night, blindfolded and with two broken feet to boot."
Bob Feller, on Tommy Henrich

OPENING DAY

"A home opener is always exciting, no matter if it's home or on the road."

Yogi Berra

"Today is Opening Day in baseball. Out in Yankee Stadium, Billy Martin just threw out his first punch."

Johnny Carson

"You look forward to it like a birthday party when you're a kid. You think something wonderful is going to happen."

Joe DiMaggio, on Opening Days

JOE PAGE

"There are two things that make Page a great relief pitcher. First, he's got a great arm. Second, he's got a great heart."

Casey Stengel

"The only thing he fears is sleep."
Jimmy Dykes, on Don Larsen

"No, and neither did that guy you had following me."
Lefty Gomez, asked by General Manager Ed Barrow if he got much sleep the previous night

"I never had a bad night in my life, but I've had a few bad mornings."
Lefty Gomez

"If I hadn't met those two at the start of my career, I would have lasted another five years."
Mickey Mantle, on Whitey Ford and Billy Martin

"Anybody who can find something to do in St. Petersburg at five in the morning deserves a medal, not a fine."
Casey Stengel, on Don Larsen ramming his car into a tree at 5 A.M. during spring training

"He went out to mail a letter."

> *Casey Stengel, on what Larsen was*
> *doing out at 5 A.M.*

"He was known to play night games no matter what it said on the schedule."

> *Vic Ziegel, on Joe Pepitone*

HERB PENNOCK

"If you were to cut that bird's head open, the weaknesses of every batter in the league would fall out."

> *Miller Huggins, on Herb Pennock*

"He didn't throw it past you. He just made you hit it at somebody."

> *Lloyd Waner, on Pennock*

"That might have been the best game you ever pitched."

> *Yogi Berra, to Don Larsen after*
> *Larsen's perfect game in the 1956*
> *World Series*

"I was too far away to see how high Yogi had to jump for it."

> *Mickey Mantle, playing center field,*
> *on the called third strike on final*
> *batter Dale Mitchell in Larsen's*
> *perfect game*

"I never had so many assistant managers in my life. Every time Larsen got ready to throw a pitch, the guys on the bench were hollering out to the fielders, telling them where to play the hitters."

> *Casey Stengel, on Larsen's*
> *perfect game*

PITCHING

"I always felt the pitcher had the advantage. It's like serving in tennis."
Allie Reynolds

"Nobody ever had too many of them."
Casey Stengel, on pitchers

"You can't have a miracle every day—except you can when you get great pitching."
Casey Stengel

PLAYOFFS

"Our fans think we've already won the World Series by beating the Yankees."
George Brett, after the Royals finally beat the Yankees in the 1980 playoffs following several successive losses

"I challenged him. He hit my best pitch. I've got to give him credit."

> *Mark Littell, on Chris Chambliss*
> *hitting the game-winning home run*
> *that catapulted the Yankees into the*
> *'76 World Series*

PUSH 'EM UP TONY

"There was no one whose hitting and fielding and hustle and fire and brilliantly swift thinking meant more to any team."

> *Red Smith, on Tony Lazzeri*

RED SOX

"All literary men are Red Sox fans—to be a Yankee fan in a literate society is to endanger your life."

> *John Cheever*

"You know, you dream about things like that when you're a kid. Well, my dream came true."
> *Bucky Dent, on his home run that*
> *gave the Yankees the lead in the*
> *'78 divisional playoff game*

"It just adds to the pinstripe tradition."
> *Catfish Hunter, after beating the*
> *Red Sox in the '78 divisional*
> *playoff game*

"Even Affirmed couldn't catch the Red Sox now."
> *Reggie Jackson, referring to the*
> *Triple Crown–winning racehorse and*
> *the Red Sox' 14-game lead in 1978*

"It was an insurance run, so I hit it to the Prudential Center."
> *Reggie Jackson, on a home run he*
> *hit in Fenway Park*

"Do the Yankees like the Red Sox?"
> *Gary Kasparov, asked if he liked his*
> *chess rival Anatoly Karpov*

"I'd hate to be on a team that goes down in history with the '64 Phillies and the '67 Arabs."

> *Bill Lee, on the '78 Red Sox, who*
> *were overtaken by the Yankees after*
> *building a big lead in the standings*

"I think George Steinbrenner used his clone money. I think those were Yankee clones out there from teams of the past."

> *Fred Lynn, after the Yankees swept*
> *the Red Sox in a climactic series*
> *during the '78 season*

REGGIE

"I sure wish that I'd had a chance to talk to him at first base, but he didn't stay long enough for conversation."

> *Steve Garvey, on Reggie Jackson's*
> *three homers in Game 6 of the*
> *'77 World Series*

"I must admit when Reggie hit his third home run and I was sure nobody was looking, I applauded in my glove."

> *Steve Garvey*

"The difference with the Yankees is guys paid attention to what he said. At Oakland, nobody listened to him. We just watched him hit."

Catfish Hunter, on all the attention received by Reggie in New York

"He'd give you the shirt off his back. Of course, he'd call a press conference to announce it."

Catfish Hunter

"When you unwrap a Reggie bar, it tells you how good it is."

Catfish Hunter

"Because I can't see myself play."

Reggie Jackson, on why he didn't like watching the World Series on TV

"This team, it all flows from me. I've got to keep it going. I'm the straw that stirs the drink."

Reggie Jackson, after being acquired by the Yankees

"Fans don't boo nobodies."

Reggie Jackson, approving the boos he got from fans

"There isn't enough mustard in the world to cover Reggie Jackson."

Darold Knowles

"I think there are going to be a lot of Reggies born in this town."

Bill Lee, on Reggie's three homers in Game 6 of the '77 World Series

"Something odd always happens around him."

Bob Lemon, on Reggie being hit by a Bill Russell throw in Game 4 of the '78 World Series

"Reggie once said that the only people he can relate to are the writers. That's because they are the only ones who can benefit from hearing his crap."

Sparky Lyle

"He passed me on the all-time strikeout list a couple of years ago and nobody asked me about that."

Mickey Mantle, asked his opinion of Reggie passing him on the all-time home-run list

"The advantage of playing in New York is getting to watch Reggie Jackson play every day. And the disadvantage is in getting to watch Reggie Jackson play every day."

Graig Nettles

"Out of what—a thousand?"

Mickey Rivers, on Jackson's claim
that he had a 160 IQ

"He's the MVP . . . and his most impressive move all night was the broken-field run he made to get back to the dugout. He could help the New York Giants."

Don Sutton, on Reggie's three homers
in Game 6 of the '77 World Series

"The only chance you've got around here is to be dead, retired, or Reggie."

Dave Winfield, on playing for
the Yankees

REGGIE AND BILLY

"If I was going to sit between Reggie and Billy,
I would have insisted on a fourth man in the
booth—[boxing referee] Arthur Mercante or
Carlos Padilla."

>   *Al Michaels, after hearing that*
>   *Billy Martin and Reggie Jackson*
>   *might announce with him during a*
>   *World Series*

RELIEF IN SIGHT

"I've come to the conclusion that the two most
important things in life are good friends and a
good bull pen."

>   *Bob Lemon*

"Why pitch nine innings when you can get just as
famous pitching two?"

>   *Sparky Lyle*

RELIGION

"No, but I saw him."

> *Yogi Berra, asked if he had an*
> *audience with the Pope*

"I guess the Old Man upstairs must have figured that everyone is entitled to one good day."

> *Don Larsen, on his perfect game in*
> *the 1956 World Series*

REPORT CARD

"I really don't deserve an A—, but you've got to understand I never got one in high school, and as long as this was an opportunity to grade myself, I couldn't waste it."

> *Joe Cowley, on giving himself an*
> *A— rating midway through the*
> *'85 season*

RETURN TO SENDER

"Gee, you've known me all these years and you still don't know how to spell my name."

> *Yogi Berra, after receiving a check*
> *that said "Payable to Bearer"*

BOBBY RICHARDSON

"He doesn't drink, he doesn't smoke, he doesn't chew, he doesn't stay out late, and he still can't hit .250."

> *Casey Stengel, on Richardson*

ROAD GAMES

"Take those fellows over to the other diamond—I want to see if they can play on the road."

> *Casey Stengel, during an*
> *intersquad practice*

ROYALTY

"Nice to meet you, King."

Yogi Berra, meeting King George V

SCHOOL'S OUT
FOR SUMMER

"Closed."

*Yogi Berra, asked how he
liked school*

SCOOTER

"What is that, the Lilliputian village? I remember
when the Yankees had a man playing shortstop.
Now they got a little boy."

*Lefty Gomez, his initial reaction to
Phil Rizzuto*

"My best pitch is anything the batter grounds,
lines, or pops in the direction of Phil Rizzuto."
Vic Raschi

'78 SEASON

"The way things were going with Billy and
Reggie and all that stuff, it wasn't a question
of *where* we were going to finish but *if* we were
going to finish."

Graig Nettles, on Bob Lemon
replacing Billy Martin as manager
midway through the '78 season

'77 SEASON

"I can't wait to pick up the paper every morning
and see what's happening. It's like *Mary Hartman,*
Mary Hartman."

Bob Lemon, on watching the
Yankees from afar as the
'77 White Sox manager

"We judge players on what they do on the field. If we wanted nine boys, we'd go on the church's step to pick up a nice collection."

Gabe Paul

"We're the Damn Yankees. . . . Except our theme song isn't 'You Gotta Have Heart'; it's 'You Gotta Have News.'"

Gabe Paul

SEX

"I'd rather hit than have sex."

Reggie Jackson

"Going to bed with a woman the night before a game never hurt a ballplayer. It's staying up all night looking for one that does him in."

Casey Stengel

"You gotta learn that if you don't get it by midnight, chances are you ain't gonna get it, and if you do, it ain't worth it."

Casey Stengel

PETE SHEEHY

"I hope the Yankees put a plaque in center field for him. He belongs out there more than anybody. He was a Yankee."

> *Billy Martin, on the death of the Yankees' clubhouse man of 59 years*

SHOWBIZ

"You got it all wrong. In the entertainment business, you would never close a show that's drawing 60,000 people a day."

> *Phil Silvers, commenting on why baseball and entertainment are different, said before the seventh game of the '55 World Series*

'60 WORLD SERIES

"We made too many wrong mistakes."

> *Yogi Berra, after the Yankees lost the '60 World Series in seven games*

"All I know is, it was the wrong one."

> *Ralph Terry, asked what pitch he*
> *threw to Bill Mazeroski, who hit*
> *the winning home run in Game 7*
> *of the Series*

'60S

"When I covered the Yankees in the '60s they had players like Horace Clarke, Ross Moschitto, Jake Gibbs, and Dooley Womack. It was like the first team missed the bus."

> *Joe Garagiola*

SLUMPS

"Slump? I ain't in no slump. I just ain't hitting."

> *Yogi Berra*

"Swing at the strikes."

> *Yogi Berra, on the best way to stop a*
> *batting slump*

"A string of alibis."

> *Miller Huggins, on what a player*
> *needs during a slump*

"You're like a mosquito in a nudist camp. You don't know where to start."

> *Reggie Jackson, on all the theories*
> *for stopping a slump*

"We are in such a slump that even the ones that are drinking aren't hitting."

> *Casey Stengel*

"When the pressure builds up, it's like being on a bus in a mudhole. The harder you press on the pedal, the further you sink in the mud."

> *Bob Watson, on slumps*

SPEED

"There was larceny in his heart, but his feet were honest."

> *Bugs Baer, on slow-footed Yankee*
> *Ping Bodie*

"My manager spent ten years trying to teach me a change of pace. At the end of my career, that's all I had."

Lefty Gomez

"Teams can't prepare for me in batting practice. They can't find anyone who throws as slow as I do."

Dave LaPoint

"You could almost walk alongside them."

Lon Simmons, announcer, on the speed of Tommy John's pitches

"Does that make me a Hart specialist?"

Ron Swoboda, on pinch-running for Yankees teammate Jim Hart

SPITTER

"I mixed it in. I didn't have my good stuff."

Rick Cerone, Yankees catcher, on throwing a spitter during a relief appearance in a Yankees 20–3 loss

"He throws it with two strikes, the batter swings and misses, then the ball goes around the infield and comes back dry as the Sahara."

Jimmy Dykes, on Whitey Ford's spitter

"Not intentionally, but I sweat easily."

Lefty Gomez, asked if he ever threw a spitter

SPRING TRAINING

"The way to make coaches think you're in shape is to get a tan. It makes you look healthier and at least five pounds lighter."

Whitey Ford, on getting in shape during spring training

STATS

"Statistics are like bikinis—they show a lot but not everything."

Lou Piniella

STOLEN BASES

"He can run anytime he wants. I'm giving him the red light."

Yogi Berra, on Rickey Henderson

"I hear the Yankees lead the league in stolen bases. But they are asking fans to return them, no questions asked."

Mike Downey

STREAKERS

"Don't know. They were wearing a bag over their head."

Yogi Berra, asked if a streaker he saw was male or female

STRIKE

"During the strike, Billy Martin stayed in shape by kicking dirt on his dog."

Bob Hope, on a baseball strike

"I was about to wave off the guy who came up to squeegee my windshield, but then I realized it was Don Mattingly."

David Letterman, during a baseball strike

"There are more games in the second half than the first."

Mickey Rivers, on why he did not want an early-season players' strike

SUPERSTITIONS

"I only had one superstition. I made sure to touch all the bases when I hit a home run."

Babe Ruth

"Superstitious? Hell, I just think it's unlucky."
> *Lon Warneke, Cubs pitcher, asked*
> *if he was superstitious because he*
> *refused to have his picture taken*
> *with opponent Lefty Gomez before*
> *the '32 World Series*

SWEET LOU

"He catches every ball he can get to. He's the best slow outfielder in baseball."
> *Sparky Lyle, on Lou Piniella*

"I'm 43 and I'm still married to a four-year-old."
> *Anita Piniella, on turning 43 the*
> *same day her husband Lou got*
> *thrown out of a game for kicking*
> *dirt at an umpire*

"I cursed him in Spanish and he threw me out in English."
> *Lou Piniella, after being*
> *thrown out of a game by*
> *umpire Armando Rodriguez*

"Sweet refers to his swing, not his personality."
Phil Rizzuto

"He took a mediocre talent to the highest level just with his intensity. . . . He got everything out of himself he could."
Stan Williams, on the baseball talents of Piniella

TEMPER, TEMPER

"The ballplayer who loses his head, who can't keep his cool, is worse than no ballplayer at all."
Lou Gehrig

"He has to learn to control himself."
Billy Martin, after fellow manager Chuck Cottier threw a tantrum

THINKING MAN'S GAME

"If you think long, you think wrong."
Jim Kaat

"When you start thinking is when you get your ass beat."

Sparky Lyle

"I've been doing my best not to think about it, but by trying so hard not to think about it, I can't stop thinking about it."

Paul Zuvella, during an
0-for-28 slump

TJ

"Tommy John is so old, he uses Absorbine Senior."

Bob Costas

"When they operated on my arm, I asked them to put in Koufax's fastball. They did. But it turned out to be Mrs. Koufax."

Tommy John

"Ask him for the time and he'll tell you how to make a watch."

Bob Lemon, on the talkative John

"Tommy doesn't belong on the Yankees. He doesn't even spit."

Jim Murray

JOE TORRE

───────────────────────────

"There won't be a hair dryer within twenty miles of the booth."

Joe Garagiola, on he and Torre becoming the Angels' announcers

TRADE WINDS

───────────────────────────

"When I retire, I'm going to ask George Steinbrenner to send me a uniform with one pinstripe on it."

Bill Caudill, on being a Yankee for 22 minutes before being traded

"Being a Yankee means never having to say good-bye."

> *Tommy John, on the Yankees'*
> *reacquiring John, Rick Cerone, and*
> *several other former Yankees*

"Every year is like being traded—a new manager and a whole new team."

> *Graig Nettles, on playing for*
> *Steinbrenner's Yankees*

"I'm still wearing pinstripes, but they don't have electrodes in them."

> *Joe Niekro, on how he felt about*
> *being traded from the Yankees to*
> *the Twins*

"Nobody knows this, but one of us has just been traded to Kansas City."

> *Casey Stengel, asked how he told*
> *Bob Cerv he had been traded*

TRIPLES

"First triple I ever had."

Lefty Gomez, poor-hitting pitcher,
on his triple-bypass surgery

UTILITY PLAYERS

"You can't get rich sitting on the bench, but I'm
giving it a try."

Phil Linz, longtime utility player
with the Yankees

"Play me or keep me."

Phil Linz, on his motto

WEATHER WATCH

"It's so cold out there, I saw a dog chasing a cat
and they were both walking."

Mickey Rivers, on a cold day

"Hot as hell, ain't it, Prez?"
>*Babe Ruth, meeting President*
>*Harding on a hot day*

WEIGHTY ISSUES

"It's a good thing Babe Ruth isn't still here. If he was, George would have him hit seventh and tell him he was overweight."
>*Graig Nettles, on George Steinbrenner*

"I know I had to get to my playing weight. But George and I just disagreed on when. He thought it was the start of spring training and I said it was the end."
>*Lou Piniella*

"There's one guy who spends all his meal money. None of it gets mailed home."
>*Bobby Valentine, on former Yankee*
>*Barry Foote*

"It gets annoying when people tell you you're overweight. You don't run the ball to the plate."
David Wells, after showing up for spring training at 250 pounds

GEORGE WEISS

"We fought over some things, but he never stopped paying me. If your checks don't bounce, why wouldn't you like the man?"
Casey Stengel, on his relationship with General Manager George Weiss

"I married him for better or worse, but not for lunch."
Mrs. George Weiss, on her husband's retirement

WHAT'S IN A NAME?

"Everybody calls me Yogi. If I walked down the street and somebody yelled, 'Hey, Larry,' I know I wouldn't turn around."

Lawrence "Yogi" Berra

"She's the first child named after the entire Yankee infield."

Argus Hamilton, on Madonna's daughter, Lourdes Maria Ciccone Leon

"My parents thought they were going to have a dog."

Sparky Lyle, on his nickname

WHITEY

"Hell, my wife would be a great pitcher with those guys in the lineup getting home runs."

Whitey Ford, on being labeled a great pitcher

"He was a banty rooster. He used to stick out his chest like this, and walk out on the mound against any of those big pitchers."

Casey Stengel, on Ford

"If you had one game to win and your life depended on it, you'd want him to pitch it."

Casey Stengel, on Ford

WINNING

"You can't win all the time. There are guys out there who are better than you are."

Yogi Berra

"The more self-centered and egotistical a guy is, the better ballplayer he's going to be. You take a team with 25 assholes and I'll show you a pennant. I'll show you the New York Yankees."

Bill Lee, on the Yankees of the late '70s

"The Yankees don't pay me to win every day—just two out of three."

Casey Stengel

"If we win, we'll own this town."

Joe Torre, said before Game 6 of
the 1996 World Series

"When we lost, I couldn't sleep at night. When we win, I can't sleep at night. But when you win, you wake up feeling better."

Joe Torre

YANKEE BASHERS

"I would never pitch for the Yankees, because they represent everything that's wrong with America."

Bill Lee

"Rooting for the Yankees is like rooting for U.S. Steel."

Red Smith

"He was the class of the Yankees in times when the Yankees outclassed everybody else."
Roy Blount Jr., on Joe DiMaggio

"You get to meet important people from all walks of life—from Joe DiMaggio to Barry Bonds."
Michael Bolton, on why he likes
being a celebrity

"I said, 'Clipper, I could be the guy who's going to break your record. If you sign this, I'll stop at 55.'"
Darrell Brown, Twins DH, on getting
DiMaggio to sign a bat for him

"There was nothing they could teach Joe D. When he came to the big leagues, it was all there."
Jimmy Cannon

"There was always Joe DiMaggio. If we had him, we could have won. But the Yankees had him, and he murdered everybody, including us."
Joe Cronin, Red Sox Hall of Famer

"I didn't think I could give them a $100,000 year."
> *Joe DiMaggio, explaining his refusal to play another year despite having the majors' first $100,000 contract*

"I'm not Joe DiMaggio anymore."
> *Joe DiMaggio, explaining his decision to retire after the 1951 World Series*

"Well, maybe somebody never saw me before."
> *Joe DiMaggio, asked how he could play so intensely in a doubleheader in the heat*

"He knew he was Joe DiMaggio, and he knew what that meant to the country."
> *Lefty Gomez, on DiMaggio always carrying himself with dignity*

"DiMaggio was the closest thing to perfection that I ever saw."
> *Tommy Henrich*

"I don't know, and I have no intention of ever finding out."

Joe McCarthy, asked if DiMaggio could bunt

"When Joe walks into a locker room—even an All-Star locker room, it's like a senator or a president is coming in. There's a big hush."
Phil Rizzuto

"It was syllables, Mickey, the syllables were all wrong."

Paul Simon, telling Mickey Mantle why he made reference to Joe DiMaggio and not to Mantle in the song "Mrs. Robinson"

"He had the greatest instincts of any ballplayer I ever saw. He made the rest of them look like plumbers."

Casey Stengel

"When DiMag hit in the 56 consecutive games, he put a line in the record book. It's the one that will never change."

Ted Williams, on the legendary 56-game hitting streak of DiMaggio

"Seeing Yankee fans up close for the first time is like waking up in a Brazilian jail."

Art Hill, sportswriter

"Of course, if you live here long enough, I guess it's only natural that you become an ass."

Bill Russell, on New Yorkers

"They never let up on you. They have no courtesy at all. They're obnoxious. The worst."

Bill Russell

"Things are definitely getting better, but I still check my mail for ticking."

Ed Whitson, on his rough treatment by New York fans

YANKEE KILLER

"I don't want revenge against the Yankees. I'd just like to skin that old guy's head."

> *Frank Lary, on Casey Stengel, who*
> *left Lary off the 1959 All-Star Team*
> *because he was regarded as the*
> *Yankee killer*

YANKEE PRIDE

"The history of the Yankees is virtually the history of baseball."

> *Dave Anderson, sports columnist*

"Putting the Yankee uniform on every day."

> *Joe DiMaggio, asked what his*
> *greatest thrill in baseball was*

"A Yankee pitcher never should hold out, because he might be traded, and then he would have to pitch against them."

> *Waite Hoyt*

"Shut up, you guys, or I'll put on a Yankee uniform and scare the —— out of all of you."

> *Waite Hoyt, on being hassled late in his career by opponents while playing for the Pirates*

"The secret of success as a pitcher lies in getting a job with the Yankees."

> *Waite Hoyt*

"Wherever you go in the world—Denmark, China, Australia—they may not have heard of the Golden Gate Bridge or Mardi Gras, but they've heard of the New York Yankees."

> *Reggie Jackson*

"What does George know about Yankee pride? When did he ever play for the Yankees?"

> *Billy Martin, on George Steinbrenner*

"The uniform is pride."

> *Larry Milbourne*

"They were to baseball what Caruso was to the Met. The best."

> *Jim Murray, on the Yankees tradition*
> *of the '20s through the '50s*

"The reason the Yankees never lay an egg is because they don't operate on chicken feed."

> *Dan Parker, sportswriter*

"Why should we break up the Yankees? Let the other teams build up to our level."

> *Jake Ruppert, Yankees owner, on*
> *their dominance in the '30s*

"Owning the Yankees is like owning the Mona Lisa; it's something that you'd never sell."

> *George Steinbrenner*

"Being in Cleveland, you couldn't root for them, but you could boo them in awe."

> *George Steinbrenner*

"If you ran a delicatessen store, you would want it to be the best delicatessen store, wouldn't you? Well, that's how I feel about the Yankees."

> *Casey Stengel, on how ridiculous it*
> *would be to break up the Yankees*

"I'll end my career as a Yankee. It's the only place. They don't remember you for playing anywhere else."

> *Dave Winfield*

YANKEE STADIUM

"All I wanted to do was grow up and play in Yankee Stadium."

> *Johnny Bench*

"Pearson, Ruth, DiMaggio, Barrow, Ruppert, throw the ball in."

> *Rocky Bridges, after Albie Pearson*
> *retrieved a ball hit to the monuments*
> *at Yankee Stadium*

"I don't want to have to go to Yankee Stadium. I would have to arm myself."

>*George Bush, governor of Texas, on the Rangers playing the Yankees in the '96 playoffs*

"There's no way they can bury 12 people out there."

>*Bob Kearney, Mariners catcher, on the 12 monuments beyond the center-field wall at Yankee Stadium*

"I still get goose pimples walking inside it. Now I think this is about the prettiest ballpark I ever saw."

>*Mickey Mantle*

"For foes their stadium was Dracula's castle. No team came in without a clutch in the throat, a sweating in the palms, a fear in the eyes."

>*Jim Murray, on Yankee Stadium*

"The Yankees are America's team. You know, Mom, apple pie, Gucci loafers, Rolls Royces."
Tommy John

"When I was a kid, I wanted to play baseball and join the circus. With the Yankees, I've been able to do both."
Graig Nettles

YOGI

"Not only is he lucky, he's never wrong."
Whitey Ford, on Yogi Berra

"Talking to Yogi Berra about baseball is like talking to Homer about the gods."
A. Bartlett Giamatti

"Yogi's face is his fortune."
Fred Stanley

"To me, he is a great man. I am lucky to have him, and so are my players."
Casey Stengel

"Maybe he can't say it good, but he can do it."
Casey Stengel

YOGIISMS

"It's like what Yogi said. . . . What did Yogi say?"
George Bell, on the Blue Jays' pennant hopes

"What's a Yogiism?"
Yogi Berra, after Phil Garner told him he used a Yogiism

"I've got three seats reserved at my show tonight. One for you, one for your wife, and one for your stomach."

Don Rickles, to Yankees coach Don Zimmer earlier in Zimmer's career

INDEX

Italicized page numbers indicate where a person is
referred to in a quote.

Berra, Yogi, *10*, 13, 14,
    23, 26, 35, 38,
    40, 43, 48, 51, 52,
    55, *55*, 56, 58,
    63, 66, 67, 75, 77,
    80, *80*, *89*, 90, 91,
    94, 95, 99, 109,
    110, *121–122*, 122
Biloxi Blues, 67
Birds, 13
Blomberg, Ron, 25
Blount, Roy, Jr., 112
Blue Jays, Toronto, 122
Bodie, Ping, 4, *96*
Boggs, Wade, *13*
Bolton, Michael, 112
Bonds, Barry, 112
Bonds, Bobby, *25*
Bonilla, Bobby, 54
Bouton, Jim, 1, 8, 11,
    14, 19, 28, 45
Bradley, Mark, 72
Braves, Atlanta, 72
Breslin, Jimmy, 4
Bressler, Rube, 4
Brett, George, 81
Brewers, Milwaukee, 37
Broeg, Bill, 4
Brown, Darrell, 112
Brown, Dr. Bobby, 14,
    27

Buck, Jack, 15
Bush, Donie, 68
Bush, George
    (governor), 120

Cannon, Jimmy, 60,
    112
Cardinals, St. Louis,
    60
Carson, Johnny, 11, 33,
    77
Caruso, Enrico, *118*
Caudill, Bill, 104
Cerone, Rick, 97
Cerv, Bob, 105
Chambliss, Chris, *82*
Cheever, John, 82
Clarke, Horace, *95*
Coaches, 19–20
Coleman, Jerry, 63
Collins, Dave, 15
Collins, Eddie, 5
Columbus, Ohio, 20
Combs, Earle, *21*
Commissioners, 21
Cone, David, *22*, 31,
    36
Costas, Bob, 103
Cottier, Chuck, 102
Cowley, Joe, *35*, 89
Cronin, Joe, 112

Raschi, Vic, 92
Ratings, 89
Red Sox, Boston, 5,
    82–84, 112
Reinsdorf, Jerry, 17
Relief pitchers, 88
Religion, 89
Reynolds, Allie, 81
Rice, Donna, *37*
Richardson, Bobby, 90
Rickles, Don, 123
Ripken, Cal, 48
Rivers, Mickey, 37, 46,
    52, 56, 57, *65*, 87,
    100, 106
Rizzuto, Phil, 8, 34,
    42, 57, *91–92*,
    102
Road games, 90
Roberts, Robin, 64
Robinson, Frank, *43*
Rodriguez, Armando,
    101
Rosen, Al, 18
Royals, Kansas City,
    34, 81, 105
Royalty, 91
Rudi, Joe, 53
Ruppert, Jake, 118,
    119
Russell, Bill, 86, 115

Ruth, Babe, 4, *4*, 5, *5*,
    6, 7, *10*, 14, *21*,
    44, *47*, *69*, 100,
    107, *107*, *119*

Schalk, Ray, 7
School, 91
Schott, Marge, *21*
Schuerholz, John, 34
Senators, Washington,
    30, *69*
Sex, 93
Sheehy, Pete, *94*
Shirley, Bob, *34*, 71
Shor, Toots, 42
Show business, 94
Sierra, Ruben, 32
Silvers, Phil, 94
Simmons, Lou, 97
Slumps, 95–96
Smith, Red, 45, 76, 82,
    111
Sojo, Ambrosio, 46
Sojo, Luis, *46*
Speed, 96–97
Spencer, Jim, 18
Spitters, 97–98
Spitting, 40
Spring training, 98
Stallard, Tracy, 60
Stanley, Fred, 121